C000170918

RECIPES

Compiled by Julia Skinner

THE FRANCIS FRITH COLLECTION

www.francisfrith.com

First published in the United Kingdom in 2012 by The Francis Frith Collection®

This edition published exclusively for Identity Books in 2012 ISBN 978-1-84589-680-5

Text and Design copyright The Francis Frith Collection®
Photographs copyright The Francis Frith Collection® except where indicated.

The Frith® photographs and the Frith® logo are reproduced under licence from
Heritage Photographic Resources Ltd, the owners of the Frith® archive and trademarks.
'The Francis Frith Collection', 'Francis Frith' and 'Frith' are registered trademarks of
Heritage Photographic Resources Ltd.

British Library Cataloguing in Publication Data

Flavours of London - Recipes
Compiled by Julia Skinner

The Francis Frith Collection
Oakley Business Park,
Wylye Road, Dinton,
Wiltshire SP3 5EU
Tel: +44 (0) 1722 716 376
Email: info@francisfrith.co.uk
www.francisfrith.com

Printed and bound in Malaysia
Contains material sourced from responsibly managed forests

Front Cover: **LONDON, THE HOKEY POKEY (ICE CREAM) STALL 1884** L130110p
Frontispiece: **LONDON, TRAFALGAR SQUARE 1908** L130152
Contents: **LONDON, CHEAPSIDE, THE APPLE SELLER c1890** L1302001

The colour-tinting is for illustrative purposes only, and is not intended to be historically accurate

AS WITH ANY HISTORICAL DATABASE, THE FRANCIS FRITH ARCHIVE IS CONSTANTLY BEING
CORRECTED AND IMPROVED, AND THE PUBLISHERS WOULD WELCOME INFORMATION ON
OMISSIONS OR INACCURACIES

CONTENTS

2   Soup

4   Fish

14 Eggs

16 Vegetables

26 Meat and Poultry

36 Puddings, Pies and Desserts

44 Teatime and Baking

54 Francis Frith - Pioneer Victorian
    Photographer

RECIPE

LONDON PARTICULAR

London used to be notorious for the dense fogs that covered the city in winter, a combination of mist and smoke from thousands of coal fires. The fogs are now a thing of the past, following the Clean Air Act of 1956, but are recalled in the name of this famous soup. The fogs were often called 'pea soupers', after the particularly thick soup that is made from dried peas. Charles Dickens, the author and great chronicler of 19th-century London, described the fog as a 'London Particular' in his novel 'Bleak House' (1852-53); in time, the two names became interchangeable for both the fog and the pea soup. When making this soup, remember to put the peas in enough cold water to cover the evening before using, and leave to soak overnight. This quantity will make enough for 4 people.

15g/ ½ oz butter
2 rashers streaky bacon, with rinds removed, chopped into pieces
1 onion, skinned and roughly chopped
1 carrot, trimmed and chopped
1 celery stick, chopped
225g/8oz split dried peas, green or yellow (although green gives the best coloured soup), soaked overnight in enough cold water to cover
1.2 litres/2 pints chicken or ham stock (ham stock is best to use)
Salt and pepper
1 teaspoonful Worcestershire sauce
Garnish to serve, as preferred – croutons, chopped grilled bacon, or finely chopped fresh parsley

Melt the butter in a large saucepan. Add the chopped bacon, onion, carrot and celery and cook gently for 5-10 minutes, until beginning to soften. Drain the soaked peas and rinse them in cold running water, then add to the pan. Add the stock, and bring to the boil. Reduce the heat, cover the pan with its lid and simmer gently for 1½ - 2 hours, until the peas are soft and mushy.

Remove the pan from the heat and allow the soup to cool a little, then process the soup in a blender or liquidizer until it is smooth. Season the soup to taste with salt and pepper, and add the Worcestershire sauce. Reheat before serving. This is nice served with a garnish of a few croutons, or perhaps some pieces of grilled bacon, chopped into small pieces, or some finely chopped fresh parsley.

LONDON, CELEBRATIONS FOR THE OPENING OF TOWER BRIDGE 1894 L130019

London's famous fog is partly obscuring the city's iconic landmark of Tower Bridge in this photograph, taken on 30th June 1894 when the bridge was formally opened with great pomp and ceremony. The flag-bedecked steamers in this view are packed to the gunwhales with dignitaries celebrating the great event.

Uniquely for London bridges, Tower Bridge is a combined suspension and lifting bridge, and its bascules carrying the roadway can be fully raised to allow tall-masted ships and sailing barges to pass through. The upper deck at the top of the towers of the bridge was originally intended as a pedestrian footway, but nowadays it is a spectacular function room from where you can watch the sunset over the Thames.

WHITEBAIT DINNERS

Whitebait are the tiny silver fry (young) of herrings or sprats, and are eaten whole, fried until crisp. Vast shoals of these tiny fish used to be caught in the Thames estuary each year between March and August, and for many centuries it was a summer custom for Londoners to travel down the Thames from Westminster Bridge to Blackwall and Greenwich to consume freshly caught whitebait at the riverside inns, where they were dipped in flour and fried. It was also a tradition for most of the 19th-century for Government ministers to mark the end of each Parliamentary session by holding a grand 'whitebait dinner' at Greenwich, a custom that lasted until 1894. The Tories (equivalent to the modern Conservatives) held their whitebait dinners at the Old Ship Tavern, which stood at the present entrance to the foot tunnel by Greenwich Pier, whilst the Liberals held theirs at the Trafalgar Tavern. The Old Ship Tavern was destroyed by a bomb in 1941, during the Second World War, but the Trafalgar Tavern still stands on the bank of the Thames, and still serves excellent whitebait dinners. The Trafalgar Tavern was also a favourite haunt in the 19th century of the writers Charles Dickens and William Makepeace Thackeray and artists George Cruikshank and James Tissot, who all congregated there for whitebait suppers. Dickens greatly enjoyed these convivial evenings, on one occasion confessing that 'There is no next morning headache like that which follows a Greenwich dinner'.

GREENWICH, THE TRAFALGAR TAVERN FROM ACROSS THE RIVER THAMES 2005 G204702

RECIPE

CRISPY FRIED WHITEBAIT

Crispy fried whitebait still makes a tasty starter or snack, but the fishing of whitebait in the Thames is restricted now, to conserve fish stocks. Most whitebait catches sold nowadays are caught elsewhere in the world, deep-frozen and available all year. If you want to 'devil' the whitebait, use Cayenne pepper instead of the black pepper in this recipe – 'devilling', adding hot, fiery pepper or mustard to food to spice it up, was very popular in Victorian times. Serves 4.

> 450g/1 lb whitebait
> 115g/4oz plain flour
> 1 teaspoonful salt
> 1 teaspoonful either freshly ground black pepper or
>   Cayenne pepper
> 300ml/ ½ pint milk
> Oil for deep frying
> Lemon wedges, thin slices of buttered brown bread
>   and tartare sauce, to serve

If using fresh whitebait, wash and dry them. If frozen, allow the whitebait to thaw thoroughly. Put the whitebait in a bowl with the milk and leave for 5 minutes (this helps the flour to stick), then drain them well in a sieve. Mix the flour with the salt and black pepper (or Cayenne pepper, if 'devilling') and put half of it in a large plastic bag. Put half the whitebait in the bag and shake it well, until the fish are well coated with the seasoned flour. Remove the fish and shake off any surplus flour. Repeat with the rest of the flour and remaining whitebait. Heat the oil in a large pan or deep fryer until it is just smoking. Add a small batch of floured whitebait and fry for 2-3 minutes, until they are crisp and golden. Lift out, drain on crumpled kitchen paper and keep hot whilst the rest of the fish are fried in batches, not too many at a time. Sprinkle the cooked whitebait with salt, and serve with thin slices of brown bread and butter, lemon wedges and tartare sauce, if liked.

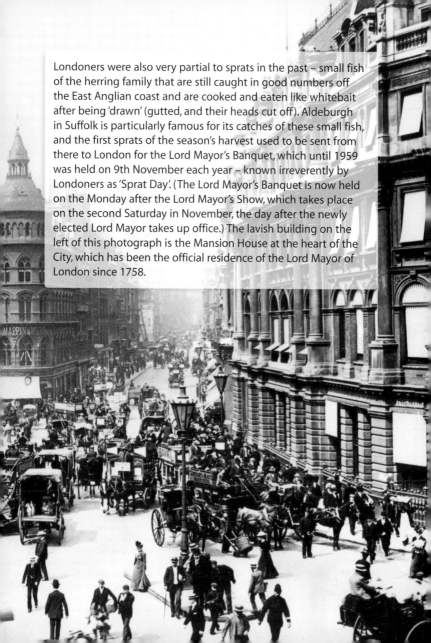

Londoners were also very partial to sprats in the past – small fish of the herring family that are still caught in good numbers off the East Anglian coast and are cooked and eaten like whitebait after being 'drawn' (gutted, and their heads cut off). Aldeburgh in Suffolk is particularly famous for its catches of these small fish, and the first sprats of the season's harvest used to be sent from there to London for the Lord Mayor's Banquet, which until 1959 was held on 9th November each year – known irreverently by Londoners as 'Sprat Day'. (The Lord Mayor's Banquet is now held on the Monday after the Lord Mayor's Show, which takes place on the second Saturday in November, the day after the newly elected Lord Mayor takes up office.) The lavish building on the left of this photograph is the Mansion House at the heart of the City, which has been the official residence of the Lord Mayor of London since 1758.

RECIPE

EEL PIE

The River Thames was once full of sweet-tasting eels, and traditional Cockney cuisine is famous for eels cooked in a variety of ways, stewed, jellied, or baked in pies. The Cockney love of eels was even mentioned by William Shakespeare in his play 'King Lear', when the Fool describes a Cockney woman making a pie, putting eels 'in the paste alive'. Eel Pie was a favourite dish of Londoners in the past, and is even honoured in the name of Eel Pie Island in the Thames at Twickenham, formerly in the historic county of Middlesex but now in the south-west London Borough of Richmond-upon-Thames and part of Greater London. In the mid 19th century the island became a popular resort for steamer excursions along the Thames from London. The eel pies served there gave it its nickname, which has stuck ever since.

    1.4kg/3 lbs skinned eels
    300ml/ ½ pint fish stock
    Salt and pepper
    1 bunch of fresh herbs
    1 tablespoonful finely chopped fresh parsley
    115g/4oz onions, peeled and thinly sliced
    1 tablespoonful lemon juice
    225g/8oz shortcrust or puff pastry, as preferred
    1 egg

Wash the eels, cut them into small pieces and place them in a pan. Add the fish stock, salt and pepper, the bunch of herbs and onions, and simmer gently until the eel pieces are tender enough for the bones to be removed. Arrange the boned eels in a pie dish, and add the chopped parsley, lemon juice and enough strained stock to cover the eels (reserve the rest in case needed – see below). Cover with a lid of pastry, brush with beaten egg and bake in a hot oven for about 45 minutes (225°C/425°F/Gas Mark 6). A little extra stock may be poured into the pie through a hole in the centre of the pastry before serving.

EEL, PIE AND MASH SHOPS

Eels are still caught in the Thames, although not in the numbers they were in the past, and live eels are still sold in London's Billingsgate Fish Market from great water-filled drawers, but eel pie has all but vanished from the city's streets and cafés. However, jellied eels – made of eels cooked and set in a jelly made from their cooking liquid – and stewed eels can still be found, either from street stalls or in the last few remaining traditional Eel, Pie and Mash shops in the city. There used to be many of these all over London and its outlying areas, selling cooked eels, minced beef pies and mashed potatoes, all of which were served with 'liquor' – a delicate green sauce made with parsley.

A famous name in the eel, pie and mash business is Manzes, started in 1902 by Michele Manze, an Italian immigrant, when he bought an existing business in Tower Bridge Road in Bermondsey. It became a family business that grew, and by the mid 20th century there were 14 Manzes eel, pie and mash shops in London. That first Manzes shop at 87 Tower Bridge Road is still there, and is now the oldest eel, pie and mash shop still in business in London. The shop still retains its traditional interior décor of white, cream and green tiles, narrow marble-topped tables and counters and dark wooden benches. Two other Manzes traditional eel, pie and mash shops run by the same family are still in business in the London area, at 105 High Street in Peckham, and 226 High Street in Sutton.

Within living memory London's eel, pie and mash shops used to display writhing live eels in their windows, often closely watched by local children eagerly waiting to see the eels dispatched by efficient beheading, then chopped into chunks for the pot. However, this is not something you see on the city's streets today.

Although jellied eels, stewed eels, pie, mash and 'liquor' are often associated with the East End of London, these traditional London delicacies used to be enjoyed all over the city and its outlying boroughs, and were part of many people's lives until quite recent times – here are some nostalgic memories about these and other foods that people enjoyed in the past which have been contributed to the 'Share Your Memories' facility of the website of The Francis Frith Collection, **www.francisfrith.com**:

I was born in 1942 and spent my childhood in Walthamstow… Ahhh – happy days! Saturday afternoons were invariably spent walking down the High Street for a bag of roasted peanuts from a stall opposite Clare's fish shop; fresh kippers from Clare's for Saturday tea; ice-cream cones from Rossi's; pie and mash at Manzes where my cousin worked, selling live eels outside – I'd watch him cut the heads off before selling them; another ice-cream from the Como Café and, finally, hot roasted chestnuts from the old man with the brazier near Woolworths. Phew – what a feast!
Roy Beiley

My family lived at 7 Newport Road in Leyton in the 1950s… I remember walking to Walthamstow to watch the eels wiggling around ice blocks at the pie and eel shop. The pie and mash with parsley sauce was the biggest treat imaginable…
Valerie Stephens

I was brought up at Brixton from 1944 until 1969… My greatest love of Brixton was the 'pie and mash/stewed eel' shop. Double pie and mash with liquor was always my Saturday main meal.
Keith Towers

There was the wonderful Harringtons pie and mash shop in Tooting, where I had the job of going on Saturday nights with my glass jar for 'licker'. It didn't seem to matter what size jar you had, they filled it up anyway. Lovely grub!
Jackie Rice

There used to be a pie and mash shop in Ripple Road in Barking that was a favourite haunt of our family. I remember being sent to the shop with a basin to buy the pie, mash and liquor – wow, that was a fantastic feast to us. I used to carry a large pudding dish and a plate to cover it with. It was my task as a young lad once a week to walk from home to the pie and mash shop to get the bowl filled with liquor (a form of sauce, best with mash potato, pie and eels). Like fish and chips once a week, pie and mash was also a delicacy.
John Willats

I loved the old Battersea of my childhood… I remember going to the Saturday morning pictures at the Granada, then to Browns Pie and Mash shop for our lunch – we used to take our own fork and spoon, our mums said you don't know who's been using theirs.
Jill White

During the early years after the Second World War my mother would take me to Woolwich from our home in Dartford as a special treat. I was about 8 years old then. We would catch the 696 trolleybus from Dartford market and arrive at the Woolwich Arsenal around lunch time. Our first stop was Manzes Pie and Eel shop – absolutely delicious after the wartime food.
Alfred Ward

I grew up in West Ham from my birth until 1960… On Saturdays we would go to the morning pictures at the Century Cinema in West Ham Lane, then we had pie and mash for lunch at Cook's, I think it was called, which had sawdust on the floor, I never understood why they did that till many years later. On Sunday mornings Titch the fishmonger would come round the streets with his barrow selling seafood, shrimps, winkles, crab, whelks, all sold by the pint, which Mum would buy as we would have that for tea on Sundays. I used to help prepare the winkles, you had to use a pin to take the black spot out of the shell, then pull the winkle out and put it into a little bowl of vinegar...
Joan Doble

11

LONDON, ST GILES
FISH STALL 1885
L130215

'COD AND CHIPS TWICE, PLEASE!'

One of modern Britain's favourite take-away meals is Fish and Chips, which was originally the street food of the poor of Scotland, the North of England and London. Both items have their origins in immigrant cookery, brought to Britain by religious refugees from Europe. Although a number of shops in the poorest districts of London were selling fried potatoes by the 1840s, fried potatoes in the form of chips as we know them today first became widely popular in the north of Britain a few years later, probably introduced to this country by Huguenot (Protestant) refugees from Belgium, home of the 'frite'. The method of frying fish coated in a flour and water batter to crisp it up and prevent the fat spitting was probably brought into Britain through London, by Sephardic Jewish immigrants from Portugal and Spain who came to the East End in the 18th century, where they ran fried fish shops – by the mid 1800s there were around 300 fish friers recorded in the city, and Charles Dickens mentions a 'fried fish warehouse' in his novel 'Oliver Twist', first published in 1838. The idea spread, and before long fried fish was being sold to eat with bread and butter or a baked potato in other parts of Britain, particularly in the industrial towns of the north.

The date and place where the combination of chips and fried fish actually originated in Britain as a take-away meal is hotly debated, and will probably never be settled. Although there are other contenders for the title from the north of England, the first combined fish and chip shop as we know it now may have been the one that was opened in Cleveland Street in London's East End in the early 1860s by a young Jewish man called Joseph Malin, who had started off as a 13-year-old boy hawking fried fish around the streets on a tray. The Malin family continued Joseph's business through the 20th century, although the fish and chip shop moved premises several times in its long history, finally ending up on the Old Ford Road in Bow, where in the 1960s it was recognized with a plaque by the National Federation of Fish Friers as the oldest-established fish and chip business in Britain.

Flavours of ...
LONDON
EGGS

This view looks along the Victoria Embankment from Charing Cross Bridge to Cleopatra's Needle, an Egyptian obelisk of 1500BC that was given to Britain in 1819 by the Viceroy of Egypt. The famous Savoy Hotel on the Strand is seen to its left in this view, which had only opened the year before this photograph was taken, in 1889. The writer Arnold Bennett stayed at the Savoy Hotel for some time in the 1920s whilst he was researching his famous novel 'Imperial Palace', published in 1930, which was based on life in the Savoy. Whilst he was staying there the hotel's 'Chef de Cuisine', Jean Baptiste Virlogeux, created a luxury omelette dish specially for him, filled with smoked haddock and cheese, a flavour combination of which the writer was particularly fond. 'Omelette Arnold Bennett' still features on the menu of the Savoy.

**LONDON, VICTORIA EMBANKMENT AND CLEOPATRA'S NEEDLE
1890** L130189

RECIPE

OMELETTE ARNOLD BENNETT

The classic version of this omelette as served in the Savoy is quite complex to make. Here is a (very!) simplified approximation, to serve 2 people as a light lunch or supper dish – half the omelette each should be quite enough, as it is quite rich and filling. Be sure to use naturally smoked haddock, without the bright yellow dye.

175g/6oz undyed smoked haddock, cooked by lightly
   poaching in milk, then skinned and flaked
1 tablespoonful freshly grated Parmesan cheese
Salt and white pepper
25g/1oz butter
6 eggs
2 tablespoonfuls thick double cream

Pre-heat the grill to very hot. Reserve one teaspoonful of the Parmesan cheese, then mix the rest with the cooked, flaked haddock and season to taste with salt and white pepper. Break the eggs into a bowl, season with salt and pepper and add 1 tablespoonful of water. Beat lightly with a fork. Melt the butter in an omelette pan (preferably with an ovenproof handle, so it can be put under the grill) and when it is frothy pour in the beaten eggs. Cook over a medium heat until the bottom of the omelette is just set, but the top is still creamy and liquid. (If your omelette pan is not ovenproof, now transfer the omelette, unfolded, to an ovenproof plate, and continue as follows.) Spread the haddock and cheese mixture over the omelette, pour the cream evenly over it and sprinkle the remaining Parmesan cheese over the top. Put the omelette pan (or ovenproof plate) under the hot grill and let the omelette finish cooking, until the top is bubbling and slightly browned. Remove from the heat and serve the omelette as it is cooked, open and flat with the filling on the top, not folded over as omelettes are usually presented.

LONDON, COVENT GARDEN 1900 L130025

Photograph L130025 (above) shows a busy market scene in 1900 at Covent Garden, in the magnificent central square designed by Inigo Jones in the 17th century. London's most important fruit, vegetable and flower market north of the Thames was located here until 1974, when it moved a few miles away south of the Thames to the New Covent Garden Market at Nine Elms, near Vauxhall Bridge. The busy market of 'old' Covent Garden was described in a 19th-century guidebook: 'All night long the rumble of heavy wagons seldom ceases, and before daylight the market is crowded. The very loading of these wagons is a wonder, and the wall-like regularity with which cabbages, cauliflowers and turnips are built up to a height of some twelve feet is nothing short of a miracle.' The market porters carried goods in tower blocks of specially-designed circular baskets on their heads, and took great pride in the number they could carry.

LONDON, MARKET PORTERS AT COVENT GARDEN 1900   L130026A

Flavours of ...

LONDON
VEGETABLES

RECIPE

MINTED SUMMER PEAS

The flower market at Covent Garden was no less frenetic – the Victorian guidebook went on to describe the activity there: 'In spring time it is occupied by dealers in spring and bedding flowers, and the pavement is aglow with colour of flower and leaf, and in the early summer hundreds of women and girls are busily occupied in shelling peas.' This work would have given the flower girls some much needed additional income. This is a delicious recipe for the first of the summer peas, served in their cooking juice with fresh mint. Alternatively, you could make it with 200g/7oz frozen young peas, or 'petit pois'.

700g/1 lb 9oz small fresh young peas in their pods
   (or 200g/7oz podded peas)
75g/3oz butter
3 Cos or Little Gem lettuce hearts, trimmed and shredded
4 spring onions, trimmed, halved lengthways and cut into
   7.3cm (3 inch) lengths
3 sprigs of fresh mint, plus 1 tablespoonful finely-chopped
   fresh mint
450ml/ ¾ pint water
1 teaspoonful caster sugar
Salt and freshly ground black pepper

Shell the peas and place them in a saucepan with the butter, lettuce, spring onions, springs of mint and water. Season with salt and pepper, and add the sugar. Bring to the boil then reduce the heat and simmer gently for about 15-20 minutes, until the peas are quite tender. Remove the mint sprigs, and gently stir in the chopped mint. Serve the peas in the buttery, minted cooking juice.

18

LONDON, COVENT GARDEN FLOWER SELLERS
1877
L130117

'FRESH WO-ORTER-CREASES!'

A vegetable that was sold in huge quantities at Covent Garden market in the past was the leafy green watercress. Watercress only began to be commercially produced in England in the early 19th century, grown in watercress beds set amidst pure, clear, fast-flowing water, typically in the chalk valleys of Hampshire and Dorset, although there was also significant watercress production in Kent, Surrey and Hertfordshire. It became very popular, and the development of the railways in the Victorian period allowed many tons of watercress to be transported to the London markets every week. Street vendors (often young girls) would then buy it and form it into bunches to sell around the city. Richard Rowe in 'Life on the London Streets' (1881) wrote of the city's watercress sellers: 'In fine weather, in spite of the general squalor of the street retailers, it is rather a pretty sight to see them flocking out of the great watercress market with their verdant basketfuls and armfuls, freshening their purchases under the sun-gilt water of the pump, splitting them up into bunches, and beautifying the same to the best of their ability to tempt purchasers. The fresh green, and even the litter of picked-off wilted leaves, pleasantly remind one of the country, in the midst of our dusty, dingy drab wilderness of brick and mortar; and there is something bird-like in the cress-sellers' cry as one after another raises it.'

A famous watercress seller in London's past was Eliza James, born in 1856, who started her career as a child of five, hawking bunches of wild watercress she had picked. In later life she became known as 'The Watercress Queen' because of her near monopoly on the London watercress restaurant and hotel trade, selling produce from the vast empire of watercress beds she owned at Mitcham and Beddington in Surrey and Warnford, Overton and Hurstbourne Priors in Hampshire. She ran her stall at Covent Garden market for over 50 years, arriving for work each morning on a watercress cart. When the Daily Mirror newspaper reported on her death in 1927, it described her life as 'as one of the most wonderful romances of business London has ever known'.

RECIPE

WATERCRESS SPREAD

Watercress bought in Victorian London was often eaten in brown bread sandwiches at breakfast time, as Henry Mayhew recorded in 'London Labour and the London Poor' (Vol. 1, 1851): 'The first coster cry heard of a morning in the London streets is of "Fresh wo-orter-creases". Those that sell them have to be on their rounds in time for the mechanic's breakfast, or the day's gains are lost.' Those in poorer homes who could not afford bread would just eat watercress on its own, which earned it the nickname 'poor man's bread'; however, watercress is a highly nutritious 'super-food' packed with vitamins and minerals, so it would at least have been good for them. This recipe recalls those watercress sandwiches of the past with a savoury spread that makes a tasty sandwich filling, either used by itself or to accompany ham, cheese or cucumber. It is also good spread on toast.

> 50g/2oz butter, softened
> About 50g/2oz watercress
> Salt and freshly ground black pepper to taste
> About 1 teaspoonful lemon juice

Wash and drain the watercress, trim off the tough stalks, and any discoloured leaves, and chop the leaves very finely, to give about 2 dessertspoonfuls of chopped cress. Beat the softened butter to a cream, and stir in the chopped watercress. Season to taste with salt, black pepper and a little lemon juice and mix well. Either use at once or put in a small container, cover with a lid or cling film and keep in the fridge until needed.

RECIPE

BUBBLE AND SQUEAK

Bubble and Squeak originated in the 19th-century as a thrifty but delicious dish that was popular with the poor of London and the south-east, made with mashed up leftover vegetables and potatoes. Originally it might also have included small pieces of leftover boiled beef or meat from the Sunday roast, but it is more usual nowadays to make Bubble and Squeak just with vegetables, and serve any leftover cold meat separately on the plate. The name of this dish refers to the two cooking stages the vegetables go through to make it – the 'bubble' of the vegetables being boiled for the first meal, and then the 'squeak' that they make whilst sizzling in the frying pan the second time round. Once a favourite dish of the poor, 'Bubble' is now found in trendy hotels and restaurants in London, although it is still very popular in the city's more humble cafes, where it is served as part of a fry-up, perhaps for breakfast, or with a slice of 'Bubble' as the filling in a bap. Traditionally the vegetables are fried in beef dripping or bacon fat, which still gives it the best flavour, but use vegetable oil instead if you prefer. Bubble and Squeak can be made with whatever quantities of vegetables and potatoes you have, as long as there is more potato than vegetables, so the recipe below is only a guide. This should make enough for 4 servings as a side dish to a meal of cold meat, or for 2 people for a light snack, perhaps served with a fried or poached egg.

4 tablespoonfuls vegetable oil, or 50g/2oz beef dripping, bacon fat or butter

1 onion, finely chopped

About 450g/1 lb leftover cooked potatoes, mashed, boiled or roasted

About 225g/8oz leftover cooked cabbage and/or Brussels sprouts, finely chopped

Salt and freshly ground black pepper

If using leftover boiled or roast potatoes, mash them roughly with a fork. Heat half the oil or fat in a large, heavy frying pan, preferably non stick. Add the chopped onion and cook, stirring frequently, until it is softened but not browned. Mix together the mashed potatoes with the cabbage and/or sprouts, and season well with salt and plenty of pepper. Add the vegetable mixture to the pan, stir it all together well to mix with the onions, then press the mixture with the frying slice to flatten it out over the pan to form a large, even cake. Bubble and Squeak should be full of lovely browned bits that give it a wonderful flavour, so you need to scrape and stir the mixture about a bit with the frying slice as it is cooking, exposing more of the mixture so it gets browned, then flatten it down again. Cook over a medium heat for 15 minutes, scraping, stirring and flattening as above, until the cake is flecked with crispy bits and browned underneath. Hold a large plate over the pan and invert the cake onto it. Add the remaining oil or fat to the pan and, when hot, slide the cake back into the pan, with the browned side uppermost. Leave to cook without stirring for 10 minutes, until the underside is brown and crispy. Serve hot, cut into wedges.

For many people, an essential accompaniment to Bubble and Squeak is a dollop of brown sauce. One of the most popular brown sauces in Britain is 'HP Sauce', which features an image of the Houses of Parliament on its label, although it is not made in London. It was invented in the late 19th century by Frederick Garton in his pickling factory in Nottingham and was popular with his customers, but Mr Garton sold the recipe and brand name to his vinegar supplier, Samson Moore of the Midland Vinegar Company in Birmingham, to settle a debt. Mr Moore launched HP Sauce commercially in 1903, to great success. Mr Garton named his sauce 'HP' as he had heard it was being served in one of the restaurants in the Houses of Parliament, introduced there by his local MP who had developed a liking for it.

Flavours of ...
LONDON
VEGETABLES

LONDON, MEN ARRIVING FOR WORK AT A THAMES SHIPBUILDING YARD c1910 L130056

Some of the men living in the East End of London in the 19th century were employed in the shipbuilding yards which once dotted the eastern banks of the Thames. This photograph shows men arriving by boat in the early morning to stake their claim to work and begin the day's toil at one of those yards; most were poorly paid casual workers hired daily. The Thames shipbuilding industry was in crisis by 1900, and the last shipbuilding yards in London closed a few years after this photograph was taken.

RECIPE

BOILED BEEF AND CARROTS

This dish from London's Cockney tradition was made famous in 1909 in the song 'Boiled Beef and Carrots' by Harry Champion, a music hall star and Cockney comedian who was very popular in East London. The long, slow cooking of the meat makes it beautifully tender. This is traditionally served with dumplings and is made with salt beef, available from some branches of supermarkets like Waitrose or Asda, and also online from a north London supplier, Hensons: www.saltbeef.com. You need to soak the salted beef in plenty of cold water overnight before making this dish. Serves 6.

> 1 joint of salt beef, silverside, brisket or topside,
>   about 1.2kg/3 lbs in weight, rolled and tied into a neat shape
> 6-8 small onions, peeled and left whole
> 4 cloves
> 2 bay leaves
> 6 black peppercorns
> 1 teaspoonful salt
> 2 celery sticks, chopped
> 1 small turnip, peeled and quartered
> 2 sprigs of thyme and 2 sprigs of parsley
> 12 small carrots, trimmed and scraped but left whole
>
> For the dumplings:
> 225g/8oz self-raising flour
> 115g/4oz shredded suet
> A pinch of salt
> 1 heaped tablespoonful finely chopped fresh parsley

Put the soaked beef in a very large saucepan or casserole dish. Add cold water to cover the meat by 6cms (2½ inches). Bring slowly to the boil, then reduce the heat, cover the pan and simmer the meat for 30 minutes, skimming off any scum that rises. Add the onions, cloves, bay leaves, peppercorns, salt, celery, turnip, and herbs, and simmer gently, covered, for 1½ hours. Add the carrots and simmer for a further hour.

Make the dumplings 30 minutes before serving. Mix the flour, suet, salt and parsley with enough cold water to form a dough, and shape it into 12 small balls. Remove the meat from the pan and keep warm whilst the dumplings are cooking. Put the dumplings in the pan, replace the lid and simmer for 20 minutes, until puffed up and cooked through. Remove the dumplings and vegetables from the pan and keep hot with the beef. Strain the cooking liquid through a sieve, put it back in the cleaned out pan and boil until it has reduced down slightly and has a good flavour. Adjust the seasoning if necessary, and skim off any fat from the surface. Slice the beef and arrange on a large, warmed serving dish surrounded by the vegetables and dumplings, and serve with boiled or mashed potatoes, handing the gravy round separately. The gravy is like a thin broth, so this dish is best served in deep plates, or old-fashioned wide soup bowls.

LONDON, THE BULL AND BUSH, NORTH END ROAD 1898 41581

Another popular old music hall song was 'Down at the Old Bull and Bush', made famous by Florrie Ford in the early 1900s. This photograph shows the original Bull and Bush pub of the song, at North End Road, on the border of Golders Green and Hampstead. This building was 'reconstructed' in the 1920s, although much of the fabric of the old building was retained in the pub that now stands on the site.

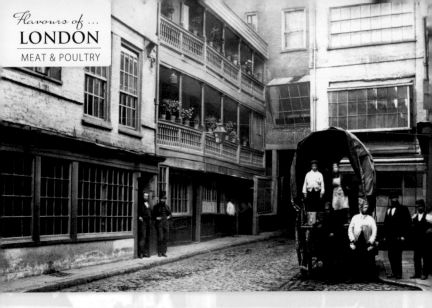

LONDON, SOUTHWARK, THE GEORGE INN c1875 L130130

This photograph shows the George Inn off Borough High Street in Southwark, London's only surviving galleried inn. Peter Wiles contributed this comment about meals at the George Inn in the 1960s to the website of The Francis Frith Collection, **www.francisfrith.com:**

'In the 1960s, the George Inn in Southwark was one of the favourite watering holes and eating houses for the young men of the accounts department of Borax Consolidated Ltd. in Victoria. In those days the serving wenches were all dressed in Dickensian costume and we would order a steak and kidney pudding. I don't mean individual puddings but a large one set in the middle of the table which was of scrubbed pine. It was terrific food and the atmosphere was great.'

Steak and kidney pudding was a speciality of many of London's inns and taverns in the past, often with mushrooms and oysters in the filling as well. As Charles Dickens wrote in his short story 'Dr Marigold', a good beefsteak-pudding 'is a pudding to put a man in good humour with everything, except the two bottom buttons of his waistcoat.'

RECISE

RECIPE

RECIPE

BEEFSTEAK AND KIDNEY PUDDING

- 350g/12oz self-raising flour
- 175g/6oz shredded suet
- Salt and freshly ground black pepper
- 450g/1 lb chuck steak, or best braising (stewing) steak, cut into small cubes
- 225g/8oz ox kidney, cored, trimmed and cut into small pieces
- 1 onion, peeled and thinly sliced
- 115g/4oz button mushrooms, trimmed and sliced
- 2 level tablespoons well-seasoned plain flour
- 1 teaspoonful Worcestershire sauce or mushroom ketchup (from condiments shelves of supermarkets)

Mix the self-raising flour with the suet, season, and add enough cold water to form a smooth dough. Reserve one quarter for a lid, roll out the rest and line a well-buttered 1.2 litre (2 pint) pudding basin. Toss the meat and kidney pieces in the seasoned plain flour so all sides are well coated and put them in the pudding bowl, adding the onion and mushrooms as you go. Pour in enough water to reach just below the top of the meat, add the Worcestershire sauce or mushroom ketchup, then season to taste. Roll out the remaining pastry to make a lid, dampen its edges and position on the pudding. Press around the rim to seal the edges well, and trim. Cover the pudding with a double sheet of kitchen foil, pleated in the middle to allow room for expansion during cooking, and buttered on the pudding side. Tie it down firmly with string. Place the pudding in the top half of a steamer over boiling water, or stand it on an upturned saucer or plate in a large saucepan filled with boiling water to a third of the way up its side, cover the pan or steamer with its lid, and steam over boiling water for 4-5 hours – longer cooking will only improve the pudding. Be sure to check the pan and add more boiling water when necessary, to stop it boiling dry.

RECIPE

YORK CLUB LAMB CHOPS

Many famous recipes have been developed for the dining rooms of the exclusive gentlemen's clubs of the St James's area of London. This dish originated at the York Club, now closed, which used to be at 8 St James's Square. It is a delicious way of oven-baking lamb chops with a crispy crust. Serves 4.

> 4 thick lamb chump chops, trimmed of any excess fat
> Freshly ground black pepper
> 1 rounded tablespoonful fresh white breadcrumbs
> 25g/1oz butter, cut into small pieces
> <u>For the sauce:</u>
> 4 onions, peeled and thinly sliced
> 50g/2oz butter
> 1 teaspoonful sugar
> 1 tablespoonful plain flour
> 150ml/¼ pint onion stock, warm (see recipe below)
> 300ml/½ pint milk
> Salt and white pepper
> 2 tablespoonfuls double cream

First make the sauce. Put the onions in a pan, add cold water to cover, and boil them, covered, for ten minutes, then strain, reserving the liquid. Heat the butter in a pan, add the onions and cook to a soft purée. Stir in the flour, and cook, stirring, for one minute. Measure 150ml (¼ pint) of the onion liquid and gradually mix it in, stirring continually until it thickens. Stir in the milk and bring to the boil, stirring all the time until the sauce is thick and creamy. Season to taste with salt and white pepper and stir in the cream. Keep warm whilst you prepare the chops, but don't let the sauce boil.

Pre-heat the oven to 200°C/400°F/Gas Mark 6, and also heat the grill to hot. Dust the chops with black pepper, place under the hot grill and cook lightly on one side only. Place the chops cooked side down in a baking dish. Cover each chop with the onion sauce, then the breadcrumbs, then dot pieces of butter over each chop. Bake near the top of the pre-heated oven for about 15-20 minutes, depending on how you like them cooked. When ready, the topping should be crisp and golden brown.

LONDON GIN

A favourite drink enjoyed in London's gentlemen's clubs as well as elsewhere in the country is a gin and tonic, and London Gin is widely considered to be the best of all gins for making this, or as a base for cocktails. Renowned for its flavour and quality, London Gin is the name for a particular blend of dry gin that gets its distinctive taste from the addition of juniper berries, citrus peel, angelica and other plants in the distilling process. There are a number of producers of London Gin, which is not exclusively made in London, but Beefeater London Gin has been distilled in the city since 1820, so-called after the popular name for the Yeomen Warders who stand guard at the Tower of London in their distinctive uniforms. They probably got their nickname because they used to be paid part of their salary with portions of meat.

LONDON, THE TOWER OF LONDON AND TOWER BRIDGE c1920
L130251

RECIPE

CORONATION CHICKEN

In June 2012 the nation celebrated the Diamond Jubilee of Queen Elizabeth II – 60 years on the throne. Her Majesty acceded to the throne in 1952 at the age of 25, and her coronation was held in Westminster Abbey in 1953, an occasion of great pageantry that was the first ever 'live' event to be broadcast on British television; many families bought their first television set to watch it. The recipe for Coronation Chicken was specially devised for the event by Constance Spry (joint principal of the Cordon Bleu Cookery School in London), and was served to the heads of the Commonwealth for the Coronation lunch with a salad of rice, green peas and mixed herbs. Coronation Chicken subsequently became a favourite dish of modern Britain, a 'new' traditional classic. It is an ideal dish for a summer lunch or buffet, and also makes a delicious sandwich filling. Serves 6-8.

1 chicken, about 2.3kg/5 lbs in weight (thoroughly defrosted if bought frozen)
1 carrot, roughly sliced
1 onion, peeled and quartered
1 stick of celery, chopped into pieces
1 bouquet garni
8 black peppercorns, lightly crushed
A good pinch of salt

For the sauce:
1 small onion, peeled and finely chopped
1 tablespoonful sunflower oil
2 teaspoonfuls mild or medium curry powder or paste, to taste
1 heaped teaspoonful tomato purée
100ml/3½ fl oz red wine
60ml/2 fl oz water
1 bay leaf
Juice of half a lemon
6 dried apricots
450ml/¾ pint good quality mayonnaise
150ml/5 fl oz/¼ pint whipping cream

Salt and pepper
50g/2oz flaked almonds (optional)
50g/2oz sultanas (optional)
Watercress or parsley sprigs to garnish

First of all, poach the chicken. Put the whole chicken in a large pan, add the chopped vegetables, bouquet garni, peppercorns and salt, and pour in enough water to cover the chicken. Bring to the boil, then cover the pan, reduce the heat and simmer very gently for 1½ hours. Take off the heat and leave the chicken to cool in the pan in its poaching liquid. Then use the chicken in the recipe as directed, but don't waste the liquid – when strained, it makes an excellent chicken stock to use in other recipes or for a soup. When the chicken is cold, take it out of the pan, take off the skin and cut or tear the meat into bite-sized chunks.

Now make the sauce. Heat the oil in a pan, add the chopped onion and cook until soft and transparent but not browned. Add the curry powder or paste, tomato purée, wine, water, bay leaf and lemon juice. Bring to just below boiling point, then reduce the heat and simmer gently, uncovered, for 10 minutes, for the mixture to reduce down by about half, then remove the bay leaf, push the mixture through a sieve and leave to cool.

Put the dried apricots in a pan with a little water, not quite enough to cover them, and simmer over a low heat until they are tender. Push through a sieve to make a purée, or process in a blender or liquidizer, adding a little extra water if necessary, then leave to cool. (Alternatively, you can add 3 teaspoonfuls of apricot jam to the sauce mixture in the above paragraph instead, before sieving it, but using dried apricots gives a better result.)

Put the mayonnaise into a large bowl. Mix in the cooled curry and tomato mixture and the apricot purée, and season to taste. Lightly whip the cream, then fold it into the mixture. (Some people also like to add a few sultanas and flaked almonds to the sauce here as well.) Add the chicken pieces and stir gently to coat them in the sauce. Turn into a large serving dish and garnish with sprigs of parsley or watercress.

Flavours of ...
LONDON
MEAT & POULTRY

LONDON, WESTMINSTER ABBEY 1908 L130150

Westminster Abbey has been the setting for many royal weddings and coronations – all but two of the English kings and queens since William I, 'the Conqueror', in 1066 have been crowned there.

Only one other British monarch besides Queen Elizabeth II has had a Diamond Jubilee, and that was Her Majesty's great-great-grandmother Queen Victoria, who celebrated her 60 years on the throne in 1897. Queen Victoria came to the throne at the age of 18 in 1837 and reigned for 63 years and 7 months until her death in 1901, the longest reign of any British monarch. She is commemorated with the massive memorial that stands in front of Buckingham Palace, unveiled in 1911. A statue represents a seated Queen Victoria facing along The Mall, and the monument is crowned by a gilded figure of Victory. Buckingham Palace is the British monarch's principal London home, and thousands of people throng to see members of the royal family appear on the central balcony of the palace at times of royal and national celebrations – especially royal weddings, when it has become a tradition for the newly married couple to share a public kiss on the balcony, roundly cheered by thousands of onlookers.

LONDON, BUCKINGHAM PALACE AND THE VICTORIA MEMORIAL c1915 L130226

RECIPE

QUEEN OF PUDDINGS

This wonderful pudding was developed in the 19th century by Queen Victoria's chefs at Buckingham Palace, who adapted it from a 17th century recipe and named it in honour of the monarch; fittingly so, as it is the most royal of puddings! This makes a large pudding that should serve 6 people.

> 75g/3oz fresh white breadcrumbs
> 3 eggs, separated
> 175g/6oz caster sugar
> 600ml/1 pint full cream ('whole') milk
> 25g/1oz butter
> Grated zest of half a lemon
> At least 3 tablespoonfuls raspberry jam
> About 1 teaspoonful extra caster sugar to finish

Butter a large ovenproof dish, at least 1.2 litres (2 pints) in capacity. In a large mixing bowl, beat the egg yolks with 25g/1oz of the sugar. Put the milk, butter and lemon zest into a saucepan and bring slowly to just below the boil. Leave to cool a little, then gradually pour the warmed milk onto the beaten egg mixture to make a custard, stirring continually until the mixture is smooth. Stir the breadcrumbs into the custard and mix thoroughly, then pour the mixture into the buttered dish and leave to stand and soak for 30 minutes. Pre-heat the oven to 180°C/350°F/Gas Mark 4. Stand the pudding dish in a roasting tin and pour in enough boiling water to come half way up its side, and bake in the centre of the pre-heated oven for 30-40 minutes, until the custard is lightly set. Warm the jam slightly in a pan over gentle heat, remove the pudding from the oven and spread the jam evenly over the top. Whisk the egg whites until stiff, then add half the remaining sugar. Whisk again until thick and glossy (but be careful not to overwhip), then gently fold in the rest of the sugar with a large metal spoon. Pile the meringue on top of the pudding, making sure that it goes right to the edge and all the jam is covered. Scatter the topping with a little extra sugar, to finish, and put the pudding back in the oven to bake for 15-20 minutes, until the meringue topping is crisp and light golden. This can be served either warm, with jam sauce or cream, or cold, with cream and perhaps some fresh raspberries.

RECIPE

HOUSE OF COMMONS PUDDING

This is also known as Chancellor Pudding and Cabinet Pudding, perhaps because it was sustaining enough to fortify Cabinet Ministers of the Government through endless meetings. Presumably all the names reflect the popularity of this pudding in the past in the dining rooms of the House of Parliament. This is best made in a charlotte tin, but a small, deep, round cake tin between 14-18cms (5-7 inches) in diameter can be used instead, otherwise a soufflé or baking dish of about 750ml (1¼ pint) capacity. Serves 4.

50g/2oz seedless raisins or sultanas
15ml/1 tablespoonful sherry or brandy
25g/1oz glacé cherries, cut in half
25g/1oz crystallized angelica, cut into small diamond shaped pieces
4 trifle sponges, or 12 sponge fingers, cut into small pieces,
   about 2cms (¾ inch) square
50g/2oz ratafia, macaroon or amaretti biscuits, roughly crumbled
2 eggs and 2 extra egg yolks
25g/1oz caster sugar
450ml/ ¾ pint/15 fl oz whole milk, or single cream
A few drops of vanilla extract

LONDON, THE HOUSES OF PARLIAMENT
1908 L130149

Soak the raisins or sultanas in the sherry or brandy in a small bowl before using, for several hours if possible, but at least 30 minutes.

Grease the tin or dish, and line the base with greased greaseproof paper or baking paper. Arrange some of the cherry halves and angelica pieces on the base, in a decorative pattern. Mix the remaining cherries and angelica with the sponge cake pieces, crumbled biscuits, the soaked raisins or sultanas and any remaining sherry or brandy. Spoon the mixture into the tin or dish, being careful not to disturb the pattern on the bottom.

Lightly whisk together the two eggs, two extra egg yolks and the sugar. Heat the milk or cream in a pan until it is just below boiling point, then gradually pour it onto the egg mixture to make a custard, stirring continually until the mixture is smooth, and stir in a few drops of vanilla essence. Slowly strain the custard mixture through a sieve over the sponge mixture, so that it seeps down gradually to the base of the tin without spoiling the pattern on the base. Leave to stand for one hour, for the sponge and biscuit mixture to soak into the custard. Cover the tin or dish with a lid made of pleated kitchen foil (to allow room for expansion during cooking), greased on the pudding side, and tie down firmly with string. Put the pudding in the top half of a steamer over boiling water, or stand it on an upturned saucer or plate in a large saucepan filled with boiling water to a third of the way up its side, cover the pan or steamer with its lid, and steam over gently simmering water for about 1 hour, until the custard is set; add more boiling water to the pan when necessary, to stop it boiling dry. Take out of the pan and leave to stand and settle for five minutes, then remove the lid and turn out the pudding onto a warmed serving dish and peel off the lining paper, to reveal the pattern on the top of the pudding. Serve with cream or custard, or perhaps a jam or orange sauce.

'CHERRY RIPE! CHERRY RIPE!'

Cherries were grown in great numbers in the counties around London in the past. They were hawked around the streets by women selling fresh cherries from their baskets, and 'Cherry ripe! Cherry ripe!' was one of the famous street cries of London.

'Cherry Pie' is Cockney rhyming slang for a lie! But this delicious delicacy is also commemorated at Wanstead, in the north-eastern London Borough of Redbridge, with an inscription on a plaque outside the George Hotel in the High Street that reads:

> *In Memory of*
> *ye Cherry Pey*
> *As cost ½ a Guiney*
> *ye 17 of July*
> *That day we had good cheer*
> *I hope to so do maney a Year*
> R.C 1752 D Jerry

Although the 'Cherry Pie Stone' is now set into the outside wall of the George Hotel, it was actually discovered inside the building when the pub was rebuilt in the early 1900s. According to local legend, it commemorates two workmen carrying out repairs on the building who leaned down from their ladder and stole a cherry pie from a pie-man who was passing by, carrying his wares on a flat wooden tray on his head. They were seen doing so, taken to court and fined half a guinea, the wording on the plaque implying that the pie was worth the expense. However, the plaque probably commemorates a feast held in the pub in 1752 that included a huge cherry pie, and was placed there by the then landlord of the George, David Jersey – whose name on the inscription has been corrupted over many years of recutting and repainting to now read 'D Jerry'. Wanstead used to be famous for its cherry orchards, and cherry pie feasts were held in most cherry-growing areas of England in the past to celebrate the harvest.

RECISE

RECIPE

CHERRY PIE

275g/10oz sweet shortcrust or puff pastry, as preferred
900g/2 lbs fresh cherries (unstoned weight)
115g/4oz caster sugar (or use more to taste, if necessary)
1 rounded tablespoonful plain flour
1 teaspoonful almond essence
15g/ ½ oz butter, cut into very small pieces
A little milk, for damping and glazing the pastry
A little extra caster sugar to finish

Pre-heat the oven to 200°C/400°F/Gas Mark 6, and place a baking tray in the oven to heat up. Roll out two-thirds of the pastry and use it to line a greased pie tin or dish about 23-25cms (9-10 inches) in diameter, but don't trim the edge.

De-stone the cherries with a cherry/olive pitter, to keep them whole, then put them into a bowl with the sugar, flour and almond essence. Mix together so the cherries are well coated, then pile into the pastry case. Dot the pieces of butter all over the filling. Brush round the pastry edge with a little milk to dampen it. Roll out the rest of the pastry and make a lid for the pie. Press all round the edge of the pie with your thumb to seal the edges well together, trim off the overhanging pastry, and cut two small crosses in the lid to allow steam to escape during cooking. Brush with a little milk, and sprinkle over some caster sugar. Place the pie on the baking tray in the pre-heated oven (this helps the pastry base to cook through). Cook for 15 minutes, then reduce the heat to 190°/375°/Gas Mark 5 and cook for a further 25-30 minutes, until the pastry is crisp and golden. Remove from the oven and sprinkle some extra sugar over the top whilst the pie is still hot. Leave to 'rest' for about 15 minutes before serving.

RECIPE

BOODLES ORANGE FOOL

This is another of the famous dishes that originated at the exclusive gentlemen's clubs in the St James's area of central London, such as the Reform, the York, the Carlton and Boodle's. Boodle's Club was formed in the 1760s, and this luscious fool has been a speciality on the menu of its dining room for many years. It is a cross between a fool and a trifle, with a sponge cake base that soaks up the creamy, fruit-flavoured mixture on top.

> 4-6 trifle sponge cakes, cut into slices about
>   1cm (½ inch) thick
> 300ml/ ½ pint double cream
> 50g/2oz caster sugar
> Grated rind and juice of 1 lemon
> Grated rind and juice of 2 oranges
> 2 or 3 orange slices or segments, and some long,
>   thin parings of orange rind, to decorate

Use the sponge cake slices to line the bottom and sides of a deep serving dish or bowl. Mix the orange and lemon rinds and juices with the sugar and stir until all the sugar has dissolved. In another bowl, whip the double cream until it just starts to thicken, then gradually whip in the sugar and fruit juice mixture, a little at a time, and continue to whip until the cream is light and thickened and all the juice is absorbed – do not over-whip the mixture though. Pour the cream mixture into the bowl, taking care not to dislodge the sponge slices. Cover the bowl with cling film and place it in the refrigerator to chill, for at least 2 hours, longer if possible, so that the juice can soak into the sponge slices and the cream thickens. When ready to serve, decorate the top of the fool with a few orange segments or slices, and a little thinly-pared orange peel.

LONDON
ST PAUL'S FROM CANNON STREET
1905 L130164

RECIPE

CHELSEA BUNS

Chelsea buns are a famous London delicacy. They were originally made and sold from the Old Chelsea Bun House in Grosvenor Row between Chelsea and Pimlico, later renamed Pimlico Road. The Bun House burnt down in 1839, but is recalled in the present street name of Bunhouse Place. Chelsea Buns have a distinctive square shape and are made from yeasted dough baked in a flat coil, rich with dried fruit and spices, and sticky with a honey glaze. This amount makes 8 buns.

For the dough:
75ml/3fl oz milk
25g/1oz unsalted butter
225g/8oz strong white flour
Half a teaspoonful salt
2 tablespoonfuls caster sugar
7g/¼ oz easy bake fast-acting
  dried yeast (two teaspoonfuls)
1 egg
25g/1oz extra unsalted butter,
  melted

For the filling
50g/2oz dark muscovado sugar
115g/4oz dried mixed fruits
  – currants, raisins, sultanas
25g/1oz/2½ teaspoonfuls finely
  chopped mixed peel
  (optional)
1 teaspoonful ground
  cinnamon
1 teaspoonful ground mixed
  spice

For the sticky glaze:
1-2 tablespoonfuls clear,
  runny honey or golden syrup
Extra caster sugar to finish

Heat the milk and butter until the butter melts. Remove from the heat and leave to cool to lukewarm. Mix the flour with the salt, sugar and dried yeast in a large bowl. Beat the egg into the warm milk, pour into the flour and work to a soft dough. Knead the dough for 10 minutes, until smooth and elastic. Return to the bowl, cover with a tea towel or place the bowl in a plastic bag and leave in a warm place for the dough to rise and double in size – about one hour. Knock back the dough and knead lightly, then roll it out to a rectangle about 30 x 23cm (12 x 9 inches), and brush with some of the melted butter.

Mix together the dried fruit, sugar, chopped peel (if using), cinnamon and mixed spice, breaking up any small clusters of currants or lumps of sugar between your fingers. Sprinkle the mixture over the dough, leaving a 2.5cm (1 inch) border around the edges. Starting from a long side, lightly roll up the dough like a Swiss roll. Press and pinch along the long seam to seal it, then turn the roll over so the seam is underneath. Shape the dough with your hands into an evenly proportioned 'log', so the buns can all be cut to the same size. Brush the dough roll with the remaining melted butter. Use a sharp knife to cut across the log, dividing it into 8 even slices, each about 3.5cms (1½ inches) wide.

Grease a large square or rectangular baking or roasting tin, just big enough to hold 8 buns quite snugly, without any extra space. Arrange the slices in the baking tin, cut side up, and spaced so they are only just touching – they swell up and press together when baking, which makes them square. Cover with a cloth and leave in a warm place for the buns to rise and double in size – 30 to 40 minutes.

Heat the oven to 190°C/375°F/Gas Mark 5. When the buns are risen, bake them in the pre-heated oven for about 30 minutes, until they are a rich golden brown. Whilst the buns are still hot from the oven, brush them with a sticky glaze of clear runny honey, golden syrup or a sugar wash made by heating up 1 tablespoonful milk, mixed with 1 tablespoonful caster or soft light brown sugar, and then brush again with a second coating. Dredge with caster sugar, and leave the buns in the tin to cool for 10 minutes before removing by running a round-bladed knife around the inside of the tin and carefully turning the whole set of buns in one piece onto a wire rack. Leave them to cool down before very gently pulling them apart into individual buns – if you do this too soon, they will all come apart. These are best eaten fresh, on the same day as they are cooked.

RECIPE

MAIDS OF HONOUR

These are delicious tarts with a rich, custard-like filling. One story about how they got their name is that they were first made by a pastrycook at the court of King Henry VIII, either for the king's first wife, Catherine of Aragon, or his second, Anne Boleyn. One day the king met a group of the queen's maids of honour eating the tarts. He was offered one and liked it so much that he ordered them to be known as 'Maids of Honour' after the ladies. In later centuries they were made and sold at a shop in Richmond-upon-Thames, now part of Greater London, and became known as Richmond Maids of Honour. The filling was originally made with milk curds set with rennet, and in later years curd cheese was used, but that is hard to find nowadays so cottage cheese is used here as a modern alternative. This should make 18 tarts.

> 340g/12oz ready-made puff pastry
> 250g/9oz cottage cheese (or curd cheese if you can find it)
> 75g/3oz caster sugar
> Grated zest of 1 small lemon
> 25g/1oz ground almonds
> 1 egg, beaten
> 15g/½ oz butter, melted, then left to cool slightly

Pre-heat the oven to 190°C/375°F/Gas Mark 5. Grease 18 small patty (tartlet) tins. Roll out the pastry very thinly. Use a straight-sided cutter 9cms (3½ inches) in diameter to cut out 18 rounds and line the patty tins, making sure the edge of the pastry comes well up the rim of the hole. Press on the bases and sides so there are no air pockets, and prick over the pastry linings with a fork. Rub the cottage (or curd) cheese through a sieve. Add the sugar, lemon zest, ground almonds and beaten egg, then the melted butter, and mix together thoroughly. Half fill the patty tins with the mixture – it is important not to over fill them. Bake in the pre-heated oven for 20-25 minutes, until the filling is risen, just firm to the touch and golden, but not over-browned. Leave the tarts to settle in the tin for 5 minutes then turn onto a wire rack to cool, when the filling will sink down a little. Serve warm or cold, dusted with a little icing sugar if liked.

RECIPE

ST CLEMENT'S TARTLETS

These little tarts with a citrus filling recall the famous old rhyme about bells of various London churches that begins *'Oranges and lemons, Say the bells of St Clement's'.* Two churches claim to be the St Clement's of the rhyme. The most likely is St Clement Eastcheap on Clement's Lane, off King William Street, and close to London Bridge. The other is St Clement Danes in the Strand. The bells of St Clement Danes actually ring out the tune of 'Oranges and Lemons', but this only dates from the early 20th century when Reverend William Pennington-Bickford had the bells restored and arranged for them to peal the tune. In 1919 Reverend Pennington also initiated a special 'Oranges and Lemons' service for children which still takes place every year in the run up to Easter, when oranges and lemons are distributed to the boys and girls in the congregation. This quantity should make 18 tartlets.

> 225g/8oz shortcrust pastry (made with 225g/8oz flour
>   and 115g/4oz fat – if using ready-made pastry,
>   you will need 340g/12oz)
> 1 orange
> 1 lemon
> 75g/3oz butter, softened
> 75g/3oz caster sugar
> 2 eggs, separated
> ¼ teaspoonful vanilla essence

Pre-heat the oven to 200°C/400°F/Gas Mark 6. Grease 18 individual tartlet (patty) tins. Roll out the pastry, cut out 18 rounds and line the tartlet tins. Grate the zest from the orange and lemon. Cream the butter and sugar together until light and fluffy. Beat the egg yolks and gradually stir them into the mixture, a little at a time so it doesn't curdle. Squeeze the juice from the orange and add 2 tablespoonfuls to the mixture, then stir in the orange and lemon zest and vanilla essence. Whisk the egg whites until they are stiff and fold them gently but thoroughly into the mixture using a large metal spoon. Pour the mixture into the pastry cases and bake in the pre-heated oven for about 25 minutes.

RECIPE

GINGERCAKE BISCUITS

A popular treat sold by street vendors in London in the past was gingerbread, or gingercake, as being sold in the photograph opposite. The black treacle in this recipe gives the biscuits an authentic old-fashioned dark colour and rich flavour, but use golden syrup instead if you prefer. This amount makes 20-24 gingercake biscuits.

- 350g/12oz plain flour
- 1 teaspoonful bicarbonate of soda
- 2 teaspoonfuls ground ginger
- 115g/4oz butter or margarine, slightly softened
- 175g/6oz soft light brown or caster sugar
- 4 level tablespoonfuls (about 60ml) black treacle or golden syrup, as preferred
- 1 egg, beaten

Pre-heat the oven to 180°C/375°F/Gas Mark 5 and grease two baking trays. Melt the treacle or syrup in a pan over a gentle heat until it is runny. Remove from the heat and leave to cool a little. Sift the flour, bicarbonate of soda and ground ginger into a mixing bowl. Rub in the butter or margarine until the mixture resembles fine breadcrumbs, then stir in the sugar. Beat the cooled syrup into the beaten egg, then stir into the flour mixture. Mix it together well to form a smooth but quite stiff dough. Flour your hands and roll small pieces of dough between your palms, to form small balls of dough about the size of a golf ball. Place the balls on the baking trays, well spaced out to allow them room to spread whilst cooking without touching each other – you may need to bake the biscuits in several batches. Bake in the pre-heated oven for 12-15 minutes, until they are risen and golden brown. Be careful not to overcook them – they should not be too hard, or too browned. Leave the biscuits on the baking trays to cool for a few minutes, then transfer to a wire rack to cool completely. Store in an airtight container.

**LONDON, A GINGERCAKE SELLER
GREENWICH 1884** L130111

RECIPE

ENGLISH MUFFINS

'Do you know the muffin man
Who lives down Drury Lane?'

Another food vendor who was often seen on the streets of London in the past was the muffin man walking along with a tray of fresh muffins on his head, ringing his handbell to let his customers know he was coming. English muffins are thick, light, yeast-raised dough cakes, which were very popular in the 19th century. They are eaten split in half, either freshly made and hot from the griddle or toasted, then spread with butter, or with jam, honey, savoury spreads, or perhaps topped with poached or scrambled eggs for breakfast. Muffins are not baked in the oven but gently cooked on a griddle, or heavy frying pan. Freshly made muffins dripping with butter are delicious. There are more complicated methods of making them, but this recipe is very easy. It makes 12 muffins.

450g/1 lb strong white breadmaking flour
1 teaspoonful salt
1 teaspoonful caster sugar
7g/ ¼ oz easy-bake fast-action dried yeast (2 teaspoonfuls)
150ml/5 fl oz/¼ pint water, warmed to blood heat
150ml/5 fl oz/¼ pint milk
25g/1oz butter
A little extra flour for dusting

Sift the flour into a large mixing bowl with the salt, sugar and easy-bake dried yeast. Put the milk and butter in a pan and warm it over a gentle heat, until the butter had melted and the milk is just above blood heat. Make a well in the flour, pour in the milk-and-butter mixture and the warm water and mix to a dough. Turn out the dough onto a floured surface and knead it for 10 minutes, until it is smooth and elastic. Put the dough back in the bowl, cover with a folded tea towel, put the bowl inside a plastic bag and leave in a warm place for about one hour, until the dough has risen and doubled in size. Knock back the dough and knead again for about 5 minutes, then roll it out to about 1cm (½ inch) thick. Use a plain (not fluted) cutter to cut it into rounds about 7cms (2¾ inches) in diameter. Place the muffins on baking sheets well dusted with flour, spaced quite well apart, and dust a little more flour over the top of the muffins. Cover with a folded tea towel and leave to rise again in a warm place for a further 30 minutes, until the muffins have doubled in size. Lightly grease a griddle or heavy frying pan and heat it over a medium heat, add some muffins and cook for 7-10 minutes on each side, turning the heat down to low as soon as they go in – this helps them cook through without burning. Cook the muffins until their bottoms are golden brown, then flip them over and cook the other side. Heat up the griddle or pan again before each batch, and turn down when the muffins go in.

Transfer the cooked muffins to a warm serving plate and wrap in a cloth to keep them hot whilst the others are being cooked, then serve split in half and thickly spread with butter. If eating later, they can be split in half and toasted. To toast muffins the traditional way, break them just a little way around their waists without opening them, toast them lightly on both sides, then pull them apart with your hands (not cut with a knife) and add butter.

This photograph shows the 'old' London Bridge which was demolished in 1968 and re-erected in the USA, at Lake Huvasu City in Arizona. In the background is Sir Christopher Wren's Monument commemorating the Great Fire of London of 1666, which started in a bakery in Pudding Lane. It raged through the city for four days and was graphically described in an eye-witness account by London resident Samuel Pepys in his famous diaries.

Samuel Pepys also recorded the drinking of tea in his diaries, a 'new' product which had only been imported into Britain since 1650. In 1660 The East India Company presented 2 lbs (900g) of tea to Charles II. His queen, Catherine of Braganza, liked it very much, making it fashionable and popular. On 25th September 1660 Samuel Pepys recorded: 'To the office...And afterwards I did send for a cupe of tee, (a China drink) of which I never had drank before.' On 28th July 1667 he commented on the supposed medicinal virtues of tea:'...by coach home, and there find my wife making of tea, a drink which Mr Pelling, the Potticary [apothecary] tells her is good for her cold and defluxions.'

LONDON, LONDON BRIDGE c1900 L130317

RECIPE

BANANA AND WALNUT TEABREAD

A huge amount of food used to be imported into Britain through London's vast docks on both banks of the Thames east of the Tower. The docks finally closed in 1981, no longer accessible for modern container shipping, and their sites have been redeveloped into the Docklands area of waterside flats, warehouse conversions and office buildings, including the gigantic office towers of Canary Wharf. The original Canary Wharf was part of the West India Docks, so named because it was the main dock for importing produce from the Canary Islands, such as tomatoes, potatoes, oranges, lemons and especially bananas. This recipe recalls the place of bananas in London's food history by using them in a teabread to enjoy with a cup of tea – afternoon tea and cakes is a treat enjoyed by Londoners and visitors alike in the city's teashops and cafes or, famously, in the stylish surroundings of luxury hotels like The Ritz on Piccadilly.

250g/9oz self-raising flour
A pinch of salt
115g/4oz butter or margarine
150g/5oz caster sugar
2 eggs, beaten
2 large or 3 medium ripe bananas
115g/4oz chopped walnuts

Pre-heat the oven to 180°C/350°F/Gas Mark 4. Grease a 900g/2 lb loaf tin, and line the bottom with greaseproof or baking paper. Cream the butter and sugar together until fluffy. Gradually stir in the beaten eggs, a little at a time, beating well after each addition. Sift the flour and salt over the mixture and mix well. Roughly mash the bananas with a fork and stir into the mixture with the chopped walnuts. Turn the mixture into the prepared tin and level the surface. Bake in the centre of the pre-heated oven for 50-60 minutes, until the loaf is risen and golden brown, springy to the touch, and shrinking slightly from the sides of the tin. Leave in the tin for 10 minutes, then turn the loaf out onto a wire rack to cool completely. Serve cut into slices, spread with soft butter, and enjoy with a nice cup of tea.

FRANCIS FRITH

PIONEER VICTORIAN PHOTOGRAPHER

Francis Frith, founder of the world-famous photographic archive, was a complex and multi-talented man. A devout Quaker and a highly successful Victorian businessman, he was philosophical by nature and pioneering in outlook. By 1855 he had already established a wholesale grocery business in Liverpool, and sold it for the astonishing sum of £200,000, which is the equivalent today of over £15,000,000. Now in his thirties, and captivated by the new science of photography, Frith set out on a series of pioneering journeys up the Nile and to the Near East.

INTRIGUE AND EXPLORATION

He was the first photographer to venture beyond the sixth cataract of the Nile. Africa was still the mysterious 'Dark Continent', and Stanley and Livingstone's historic meeting was a decade into the future. The conditions for picture taking confound belief. He laboured for hours in his wicker dark-room in the sweltering heat of the desert, while the volatile chemicals fizzed dangerously in their trays. Back in London he exhibited his photographs and was 'rapturously cheered' by members of the Royal Society. His reputation as a photographer was made overnight.

VENTURE OF A LIFE-TIME

By the 1870s the railways had threaded their way across the country, and Bank Holidays and half-day Saturdays had been made obligatory by Act of Parliament. All of a sudden the working man and his family were able to enjoy days out, take holidays, and see a little more of the world.

With typical business acumen, Francis Frith foresaw that these new tourists would enjoy having souvenirs to commemorate their days out. For the next thirty years he travelled the country by train and by pony and trap, producing fine photographs of seaside resorts and beauty spots that were keenly bought by millions of Victorians. These prints were painstakingly pasted into family albums and pored over during the dark nights of winter, rekindling precious memories of summer excursions. Frith's studio was soon supplying retail shops all over the country, and by 1890 F Frith & Co had become the greatest specialist photographic publishing company in the world, with over 2,000 sales outlets, and pioneered the picture postcard.

FRANCIS FRITH'S LEGACY

Francis Frith had died in 1898 at his villa in Cannes, his great project still growing. By 1970 the archive he created contained over a third of a million pictures showing 7,000 British towns and villages.

Frith's legacy to us today is of immense significance and value, for the magnificent archive of evocative photographs he created provides a unique record of change in the cities, towns and villages throughout Britain over a century and more. Frith and his fellow studio photographers revisited locations many times down the years to update their views, compiling for us an enthralling and colourful pageant of British life and character.

We are fortunate that Frith was dedicated to recording the minutiae of everyday life. For it is this sheer wealth of visual data, the painstaking chronicle of changes in dress, transport, street layouts, buildings, housing and landscape that captivates us so much today, offering us a powerful link with the past and with the lives of our ancestors.

Computers have now made it possible for Frith's many thousands of images to be accessed almost instantly. The archive offers every one of us an opportunity to examine the places where we and our families have lived and worked down the years. Its images, depicting our shared past, are now bringing pleasure and enlightenment to millions around the world a century and more after his death.

For further information visit: www.francisfrith.com

INTERIOR DECORATION

Frith's photographs can be seen framed and as giant wall murals in thousands of pubs, restaurants, hotels, banks, retail stores and other public buildings throughout Britain. These provide interesting and attractive décor, generating strong local interest and acting as a powerful reminder of gentler days in our increasingly busy and frenetic world.

FRITH PRODUCTS

All Frith photographs are available as prints and posters in a variety of different sizes and styles. In the UK we also offer a range of other gift and stationery products illustrated with Frith photographs, although many of these are not available for delivery outside the UK – see our web site for more information on the products available for delivery in your country.

THE INTERNET

Over 100,000 photographs of Britain can be viewed and purchased on the Frith web site. The web site also includes memories and reminiscences contributed by our customers, who have personal knowledge of localities and of the people and properties depicted in Frith photographs. If you wish to learn more about a specific town or village you may find these reminiscences fascinating to browse. Why not add your own comments if you think they would be of interest to others? See **www.francisfrith.com**

PLEASE HELP US BRING FRITH'S PHOTOGRAPHS TO LIFE

Our authors do their best to recount the history of the places they write about. They give insights into how particular towns and villages developed, they describe the architecture of streets and buildings, and they discuss the lives of famous people who lived there. But however knowledgeable our authors are, the story they tell is necessarily incomplete.

Frith's photographs are so much more than plain historical documents. They are living proofs of the flow of human life down the generations. They show real people at real moments in history; and each of those people is the son or daughter of someone, the brother or sister, aunt or uncle, grandfather or grandmother of someone else. All of them lived, worked and played in the streets depicted in Frith's photographs.

We would be grateful if you would give us your insights into the places shown in our photographs: the streets and buildings, the shops, businesses and industries. Post your memories of life in those streets on the Frith website: what it was like growing up there, who ran the local shop and what shopping was like years ago; if your workplace is shown tell us about your working day and what the building is used for now. Read other visitors' memories and reconnect with your shared local history and heritage. With your help more and more Frith photographs can be brought to life, and vital memories preserved for posterity, and for the benefit of historians in the future.

Wherever possible, we will try to include some of your comments in future editions of our books. Moreover, if you spot errors in dates, titles or other facts, please let us know, because our archive records are not always completely accurate—they rely on 140 years of human endeavour and hand-compiled records. You can email us using the contact form on the website.

Thank you!

For further information, trade, or author enquiries
please contact us at the address below:

**The Francis Frith Collection, Oakley Business Park,
Wylye Road, Dinton, Wiltshire SP3 5EU England.**
Tel: +44 (0)1722 716 376 Fax: +44 (0)1722 716 881
e-mail: sales@francisfrith.co.uk **www.francisfrith.com**